EARTH UNDER ATTACK!

EARTHQUAKE SHATTERS COUNTRY

Louise and Richard Spilsbury

Gareth Stevens
PUBLISHING

Please visit our website, **www.garethstevens.com**. For a free color catalog of all our high-quality books, call toll free 1-800-542-2595 of fax 1-877-542-2596.

Cataloging-in-Publication Data

Names: Spilsbury, Louise. | Spilsbury, Richard.
Title: Earthquake shatters country / Louise and Richard Spilsbury.
Description: New York : Gareth Stevens Publishing, 2018. | Series: Earth under attack! | Includes index.
Identifiers: ISBN 9781538212981 (pbk.) | ISBN 9781538213001 (library bound) | ISBN 9781538212998 (6 pack)
Subjects: LCSH: Earthquakes--Juvenile literature. | Natural disasters--Juvenile literature.
Classification: LCC QE521.3 S67 2018 | DDC 551.22--dc23

First Edition

Published in 2018 by
Gareth Stevens Publishing
111 East 14th Street, Suite 349
New York, NY 10003

Copyright © 2018 Gareth Stevens Publishing

Produced for Gareth Stevens by Calcium
Editors: Sarah Eason and Jennifer Sanderson
Designers: Jeni Child and Simon Borrough
Picture researcher: Rachel Blount

Picture credits: Cover: Shutterstock: Antonio Nardelli top, NigelSpiers bottom; Inside: Shutterstock: 3Dsculptor 38, Andrey VP 25, Robert Ang 21, Arindambanerjee 34, 35, Atdigit 43, Austinding 7, Jason Batterham 16, Bertl23 24, Billion Photos 9, Deepspace 30, Dutourdumonde Photography 33, Stefano Ember 12, Fabiodevilla 32, Peter Hermes Furian 14, Gonzalo Jara 39, A Katz 6, Knovakov 5, Alexander Mazurkevich 44, Mffoto 37, mTaira 13, 15, Myszka 40, Naeblys 10, Antonio Nardelli 31, NigelSpiers 22, Nonchanon 45, Prometheus72 18, 19, Dewi Putra 41, Kristin Ruhs 29, Tinnaporn Sathapornnanont 17, Think4photop 26, 27, Ververidis Vasilis 42; Wikimedia Commons: Ikluft 11, United States Geological Survey 23.

All rights reserved. No part of this book may be reproduced in any form without permission from the publisher, except by a reviewer.

Printed in China

CPSIA compliance information: Batch #CW18GS:
For further information contact Gareth Stevens, New York, New York at 1-800-542-2595.

CONTENTS

CHAPTER 1
When the Earth Quakes 4

CHAPTER 2
Planetary Power 8

CHAPTER 3
Quake Zones 14

CHAPTER 4
Shock Waves 20

CHAPTER 5
After the Quake 28

CHAPTER 6
Living in a Quake Zone 36

GLOSSARY 46

FOR MORE INFORMATION 47

INDEX 48

CHAPTER 1

WHEN THE EARTH QUAKES

Earthquakes are one the deadliest natural **hazards** in the world. An earthquake is a sudden, fast shaking of Earth caused by the shifting of rock beneath its surface. Large earthquakes can strike without warning at any time of the year and any time of the day or night. When earthquakes are unexpected like this, the results can be catastrophic.

Earthquake Alert!

Several million earthquakes happen around the world every year. Most are so small that people barely notice them happening. Annually, about 50,000 earthquakes are large enough for people to notice, even if they feel only a mild trembling beneath their feet. Of these, around 100 are big enough to cause substantial damage if they happen near villages, towns, and cities. The most dangerous earthquakes of all, huge, violent, and potentially very destructive earthquakes, occur on average about once per year. Over the centuries, these quakes have killed millions of people and have caused an amount of damage to property that is too great to be calculated.

Feel the Impact

Larger earthquakes can be felt over long distances, and they can transform countries in an instant. When a big earthquake strikes, people nearby may feel a sudden large jolt of the building they are in or the ground they are standing on, followed quickly by violent shaking. This may last only seconds or a minute or longer, but it can feel like a very long time when you are in the middle of an earthquake. The shaking or cracking ground can knock people down and cause buildings, bridges, and roads to crumble or fall. The noise can be incredible, too.

4

The energy released from an earthquake can be up to 10,000 times more powerful than the first **atomic bomb**. The devastating 2015 earthquake in Nepal left thousands of people homeless.

DEADLY DATA

Did you know that 45 US states and territories are at moderate to very high risk of earthquakes?

Shattered Countries

When an earthquake hits, it can shatter large areas of a country. Earthquakes can wreak havoc in **rural** areas, where they flatten farm buildings and damage the roads and railroad lines that provide access to the countryside. In cities, an earthquake becomes lethal when the shaking or cracking of the earth makes buildings and other structures fall. There are other dangers, too. During an earthquake, people also face the threat of being drowned in a flood, becoming buried under a **landslide**, or being burned in a fire.

Shaking and Cracking

One of the most dangerous hazards of an earthquake is the shaking ground. The shaking itself damages buildings and other structures, and then, when the shaking stops, the ground often settles at a different level than it was before. This is called subsidence. Subsidence causes buildings to crumble. An earthquake can also make the ground heave and lurch, making anything in its path lean or tip over. If the earth cracks below a building during an earthquake, this can rip structures apart and even cut roads in half.

Building inspectors figure out what to do with a collapsed office structure after an earthquake destroyed buildings in Los Angeles, California, in 1994.

> Earthquakes cause dangerous hazards when they crack and wreck roads, and topple or snap power lines.

Floods and Fires

Few people realize that earthquakes can also cause floods and fires. If a quake **ruptures** the **dams** or **levees** along a river, the water from the river or **reservoir** then floods the surrounding land, damaging or washing away buildings and drowning people. Fires happen if the shaking ground breaks gas and electrical power lines, or knocks over wood or coal stoves. Such fires become even deadlier if the quake has broken water pipes to fire hydrants that could help people extinguish the fires.

Under Attack

In an earthquake, it can really feel as if a country is under attack on all fronts. The shaking ground can trigger landslides, **mudslides**, and **avalanches** on steeper hills or mountains. When a quake judders and loosens piles of rock, mud, and snow on a slope, they hurtle downhill quickly and can damage or bury buildings, or even entire villages, below. These landslides are often more destructive than the actual earthquakes.

EARTH UNDER ATTACK!

> During an earthquake, when gas lines are broken, gas is set free, and the slightest spark can start a fire that can turn into a raging inferno.

CHAPTER 2

PLANETARY POWER

To find out what causes earthquakes, we have to journey deep into the center of Earth. Earthquakes happen because of the way Earth is made and the incredible power and energy that is at work deep beneath the surface rock that we live on. Seismology is the scientific study of all aspects of earthquakes, and **seismologists** have found the answers to questions such as why and how earthquakes occur.

Layers of Earth

Our planet has four major layers: the inner core, outer core, mantle, and crust. The inner core is the central, hottest part of Earth. After the inner core is the outer core. This layer is made of mostly molten (melted) metals, including nickel and iron. The mantle is the thick layer of sticky, incredibly hot rock beneath Earth's crust. The crust is Earth's surface, or outer, layer. It is made up of hard rock that is between 4 and 50 miles (6 and 80 km) deep in different places. The crust forms the land on which we live and the floor of the oceans. Millions of years ago, this layer of rock cracked and split into many pieces, like a puzzle, covering Earth's surface. These huge pieces of flat rock are called **tectonic plates**.

Melting Rock

Although we cannot feel the ground moving beneath our feet, Earth's tectonic plates are constantly, but very slowly, shifting. They move because hot, semiliquid rock, called **magma**, is moving beneath them. The heat from Earth's core heats the mantle layer to 1,652° Fahrenheit (900° C). This temperature is high enough to melt rock. Hot magma rises to the surface in the mantle underneath the crust, and it eventually sinks back toward the core as it cools, creating movement. The tectonic plates float like enormous rafts on the magma. As they move, they scrape, bump, or drag along each other, causing earthquakes.

The inner core reaches extreme temperatures of 9,932° Fahrenheit (5,500° C). The outer core is 1,243 miles (2,000 km) thick and is a liquid. The mantle is semimolten and about 1,864 miles (3,000 km) thick.

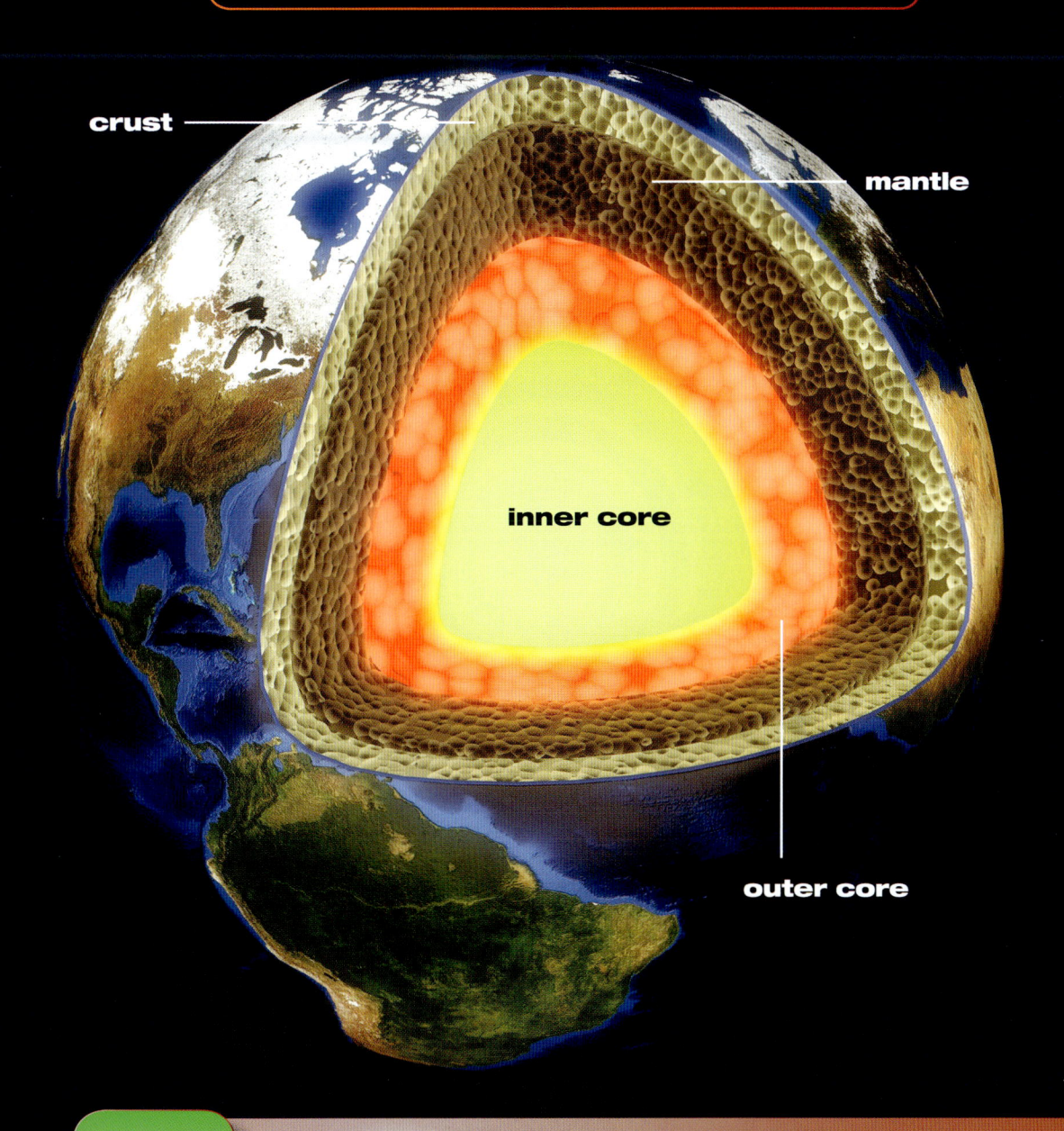

- crust
- mantle
- inner core
- outer core

EARTH UNDER ATTACK!

We feel like the ground beneath our feet is solid, but the crust is a thin layer. If Earth were the size of an apple, the crust would be as thick as the apple skin.

Battle of the Giants

Most tectonic plates move as slowly as the time it takes your fingernails to grow—just 1 to 2 inches (2.5 to 5 cm) every year! However, when these rocky giants clash, they unleash devastating amounts of energy and power. Tectonic plates move in different directions and clash in different ways to cause the earthquakes that send waves of panic and destruction through countries across the world. Some are moving toward each other, some are moving apart, and some are sliding past each other. The lines where tectonic plates meet are called plate boundaries.

Battle of the Boundaries

There are three main types of plate boundary: **divergent**, **convergent**, and **transform**. Large and small earthquakes can happen at all three types of boundary. At divergent boundaries, plates are moving away from one another. This creates gaps in the ocean floor called mid-ocean ridges, or cracks in the land, which are called rift valleys. At convergent boundaries, plates are moving toward one another and pushing against each other or sliding over each other. Earthquakes also happen at transform boundaries, where plates are moving and grinding past each other. This kind of boundary results in a crack or fracture in Earth's crust and is called a **fault**.

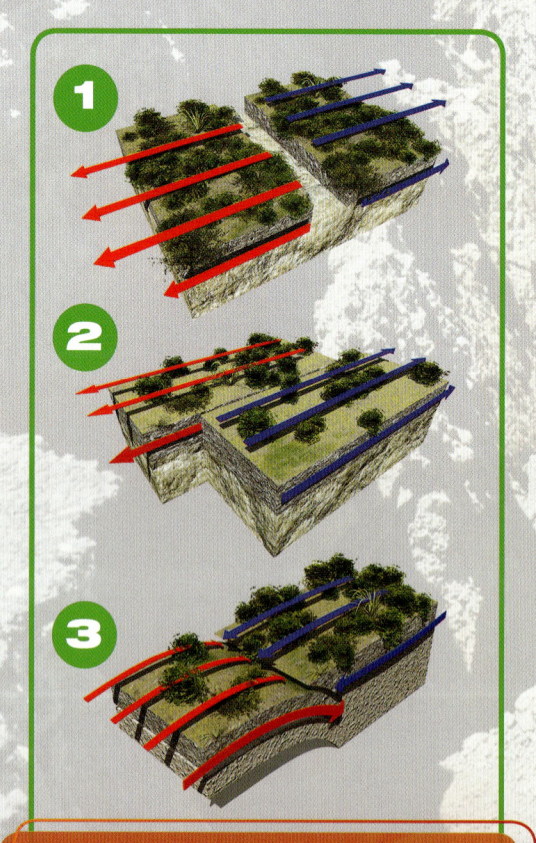

Earth's giant tectonic plates can cause earthquakes as they move away from each other at a divergent boundary (1), along, past each other at a transform boundary (2), or move toward each other at a convergent boundary (3).

Fearsome Friction

Transform boundaries and faults cause many earthquakes because the edges of tectonic plates are jagged and not smooth. Sometimes, when the plates slide past each other, the jagged edges on either plate catch and become stuck together for a time. The plates still try to keep moving, so the energy that should be making the plates move is stored instead. The energy that builds up where these two giants meet is enormous. All of this stored energy is released when the plates finally overcome the **friction** holding them together and suddenly slip into new positions. This energy passes through the plates, causing the dramatic tremors and shaking of the ground that create an earthquake.

> We cannot see where most tectonic plates meet because they are underground, but the San Andreas Fault runs down the west coast of the United States. It runs around 800 miles (1,300 km) through northern and southern California.

EARTH UNDER ATTACK!

The motion of the plates at a transform boundary has given this type of fault another name: a **strike-slip fault**. The most famous and best-studied strike-slip fault in the world is the San Andreas Fault in California.

Earthquakes Under the Sea

When earthquakes make the land shake and shatter, they cause buildings to collapse and landslides to happen. When they occur on the ocean floor, they set off a different kind of disaster, but one that can be just as deadly and destructive, and just as capable of destroying a country. An earthquake on the ocean floor can cause a huge wave called a tsunami. Most tsunamis are caused by earthquakes making the ground shake or split at the bottom of the ocean.

An earthquake on the ocean floor set off a deadly tsunami in the Indian Ocean on December 26, 2004, which caused disaster in several countries including Sri Lanka.

Killer Waves

Some people call tsunamis tidal waves, but these huge waves have nothing to do with the tides on the ocean. Many tsunamis happen because of movements at plate boundaries on the ocean floor. When one tectonic plate sticks and then suddenly slips down beneath, seawater is sucked into the gap. This sudden movement of millions of tons of seawater creates a series of waves at the ocean's surface that can become a tsunami. Tsunami waves can travel quickly over vast distances through deep water, where they may be barely noticeable. However, as a tsunami moves closer to the land, where the water gets shallower, its waves slow down and pile up, often building to great heights by the time they crash into the shore.

Crashing into Coastlines

Some tsunamis are huge. They can be many feet above the normal level of the sea. When they hit the shore, they can do incredible damage to the coastline. They can crash onto land with the same power as a fast-moving wall of concrete. They can submerge people, animals, buildings, and farms underwater. They can carry boats, vehicles, and parts of buildings miles inland. Entire coastlines of a country or whole islands can be altered by a tsunami.

> A powerful undersea earthquake off the coast of Japan in 2011 caused a series of tsunami waves that killed 19,300 people and flooded many towns and villages along the coast.

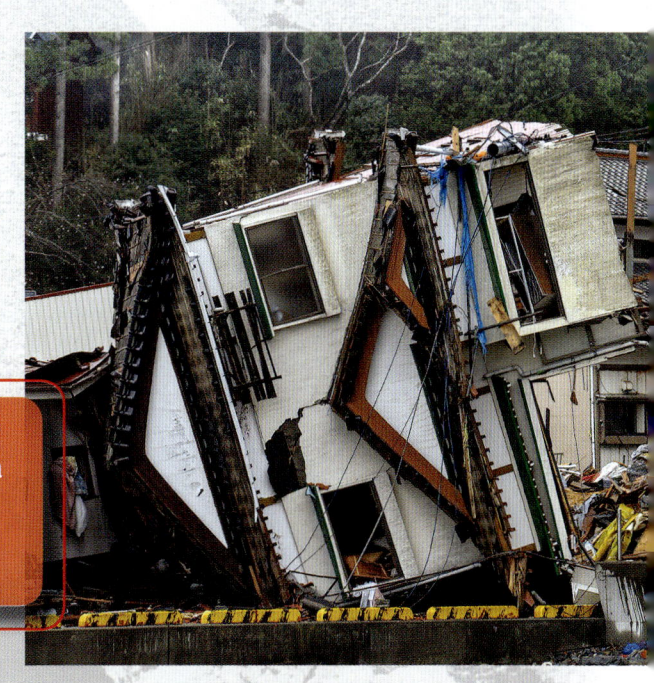

EARTH UNDER ATTACK!

Seiches are like small tsunamis. They happen on lakes that are shaken by an earthquake. Most seiches are only a few feet high, but they can still flood or knock down houses and tip over trees along the lakeshore.

CHAPTER 3
QUAKE ZONES

Historical records show that earthquakes are most common in one main region of the planet. This is where tectonic plates bash into and scrape against each other beneath the surface.

Ring of Fire

More than 80 percent of earthquakes happen in a belt of coastal land forming a rough horseshoe shape around the Pacific Ocean. The belt is often called the **Ring of Fire** because not only earthquakes but also many major, burning-hot **volcanic eruptions** occur here. The Ring of Fire is where the mighty Pacific plate beneath the ocean meets other tectonic plates beneath continents and other landmasses.

Plate Meets Plate

These plates include the North American and South American plates, the Eurasian plate, and the Australian and the Filipino plates. The plates mostly clash at convergent boundaries but at a few transform boundaries, too. For example, the Pacific and North American plates strike slip along the Californian coast, but they converge near Alaska. Some of the deepest ocean trenches are found where the Pacific plate dips beneath the continental plates.

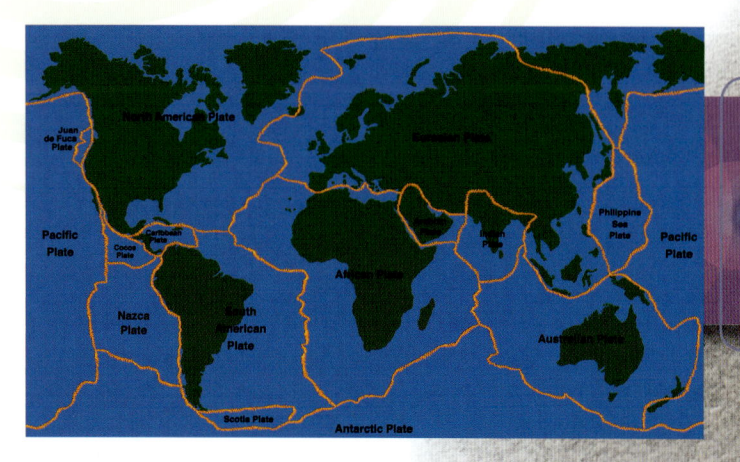

This world map shows the fault lines around the major and minor tectonic plates below Earth's crust.

People living in Japan in the Ring of Fire are at permanent risk from earthquakes, big or small.

Giant Ring

The Ring of Fire belt is enormous. It runs north from the base of Chile to Alaska. It then turns south below Siberia passing Japan, the Philippines, and finally to New Zealand. In total, the Ring measures nearly 25,000 miles (40,234 km). Any place along the belt is at risk of earthquakes, and there have been many immense and destructive events over the years. For example, the world's deadliest earthquake happened in the Ring of Fire in Peru in 1970, when 70,000 people died.

EARTH UNDER ATTACK!

Earthquakes are not the only natural disasters to occur in the Ring of Fire. Volcanoes happen in the Ring of Fire because a seawater-soaked oceanic plate dips beneath drier, lighter continental plates. The water and other chemicals in the oceanic plate combine to melt the mantle, forming magma that rises to the surface at volcanoes.

15

Where Else Earthquakes Strike

Although living away from the Ring of Fire is safer, no one is safe from earthquakes! Few people on Earth live in places where there are never any rumblings beneath the ground. Earthquakes do not always happen where plate meets plate. They can happen in mid-plate, too. However, there is another part of our planet where the chances of experiencing an earthquake are very high.

Battle of the Boundaries

If you look at a world map, you might see that it is possible to trace a rough line running west to east connecting the major mountain ranges. These start with the mightiest mountains of all, the Himalayas in Nepal and Tibet, Asia. The line continues through the Pamirs in Pakistan, the Caucasus and Carpathians in Eastern Europe, the Apennines, Pyrenees, and then the Alps. It finishes in Morocco with the Atlas Mountains. This long line is known as the Alpides earthquake belt. The Alpides is happening because the African, Arabian, and Indian plates are pressing northward into the Eurasian plate. Around 17 percent of earthquakes on Earth happen in this belt, including the deadly 1968 Iran earthquake in which 11,000 people died.

Earthquakes can happen anywhere, even places such as Scarborough in the UK, where there was a 3.8-magnitude quake in January 2017.

EARTH UNDER ATTACK!

The Alpides earthquake belt is home to many mountain chains, such as the Himalayas, which are growing taller each year. This happens because converging continental plates crumple up the crust, so it stands taller. The crumpling of solid rock builds pressure underground that is eventually released as earthquakes.

The Himalayan Mountains lie in the Alpides earthquake belt, which accounts for about 17 percent of the world's largest earthquakes.

When Do Quakes Happen?

Earthquakes can catch anyone by surprise. That is because they can happen at any time of day, at any time of the year. They do not depend on what is happening to the weather or the tides, the position of the sun relative to Earth, or other natural factors. Instead, an earthquake happens as a result of slow processes underground, such as the gradual buildup of pressure in giant chunks of rock. That is why scientists cannot predict with any accuracy when an earthquake will strike.

Disaster Report:
2011, Van, Turkey

It was just after lunchtime on a cold fall day, when an enormous earthquake struck the city of Van. This city of 1 million people and its neighbor Ercis are in the far east of Turkey. The quake came out of the blue, but **geologists** were not surprised that such a disaster occurred in the Alpides earthquake belt.

A rescue team searches for wounded under the debris after the Van earthquake.

Plate Junction

Van lies close to one of the most tectonically complex areas on Earth. It is on the North Anatolian fault, where the Arabian and Anatolian plates edge beneath the Eurasian plate by nearly 1 inch (2.5 cm) per year. It is also near the junction of the Arabian and African plates. The giant earthquake happened some 12 miles (19 km) underground, and its shaking was felt as far away as southern Russia and Jordan in the Middle East.

Earthquake Zone

The quake caused both horizontal and vertical ground movements. In some villages, there was total destruction as the mainly mud-brick homes fell apart. In the city of Van, the shaking collapsed many small apartment buildings and hotels. Hundreds of people were crushed or hit by falling bricks. The number of injured people rose quickly in the hours after the quake. Its effects were made worse because the Van region is high on a **plateau** fringed with snow-capped mountains, and winter had arrived. Both survivors and the injured struggled to survive out in the cold on the first night.

The horror of the situation was made even worse by a series of further small earthquakes, as the rocks underground settled down again. The Turkish army was deployed to search for survivors in the devastated region, and despite the isolation, help soon arrived from nearby settlements.

DEADLY DATA

The Van earthquake caused a death toll of 604 people. More than 2,500 people were injured, and thousands of structures were destroyed.

After the disaster, many people's homes were ruined and had to be rebuilt.

CHAPTER 4

SHOCK WAVES

In an earthquake, the energy released spreads out in all directions. It travels in the form of **shock waves** (or seismic waves), which work like the ripples on a pond when you throw a stone into the middle. These shock waves shake the earth as they move through it. When they hit Earth's surface, they shake the ground and anything on it. The worst shaking is felt and the most damage is caused nearest the epicenter, the place where the earthquake started.

Shocking News

Earthquakes do not send out just one set of shock waves. Many earthquakes have foreshocks. These are smaller earthquakes that happen before a larger earthquake and in the same place as the larger earthquake that follows. We can call these "shock waves" only after a larger earthquake has actually happened. The main earthquake that creates the largest shock waves is called the main shock. However powerful they are, main shocks are always followed by aftershocks. Aftershocks are smaller earthquakes that happen after the main shock and in the same area as the main shock.

Ground Shaking

The shaking caused by shock waves can damage buildings or cause them to collapse. The intensity of ground shaking and the amount of damage an earthquake causes depends on how big the earthquake is, how long the shocks continue for, and what the local **geology** of the place is like—for example, how solid a layer of rock there is near the surface. The shock waves are biggest close to large earthquakes. Since these are waves of energy and they use energy to travel farther, they become weaker the farther they go, and the intensity of the shaking decreases. So, the amount of damage shock waves do also depends on how far away a place is from the earthquake's epicenter.

An earthquake's shock waves spread through the ground like these ripples on the water.

EARTH UNDER ATTACK! ▶

Bigger earthquakes tend to produce larger aftershocks. Aftershocks can continue for weeks, months, or even years after a major main shock.

Tremors!

There is one thing possibly even more terrifying than the ground beneath your feet shaking and juddering violently, and that is when the ground suddenly turns from a solid layer to a soft, wobbling mass. When this happens, the ground may no longer be firm enough to hold the weight of the building you are standing in. This is the bizarre, but not uncommon, effect of an earthquake called liquefaction, where the ground starts to behave like a liquid rather than a solid.

Swallowed Up by the Land

When earthquakes turn solid land to liquid beneath a building, that building may start to lean or tip over as its foundations wobble and sink. Buildings topple, and cars and other vehicles can be swallowed up by the ground if soil liquefaction occurs. Mexico City is built on a former lake made up of soft **sediment**. In the earthquake that occurred there in 1985, the wet sand that the city's tall buildings rested upon turned to liquid, causing terrible damage and killing thousands of people.

Construction workers remove tons of liquefied soil after earthquakes in 2011 in Christchurch, New Zealand.

Losing Ground!

Liquefaction does not happen in areas of hard rock. It happens in areas where the land is made up of loose sediment, such as sand or soil. For one thing, solid layers of rock are less likely to shake than loose sediment. Shock waves usually shake soft, loose layers of sediment more and for longer than they shake areas of hard rock. The real problem, however, is water. Liquefaction happens when sand or soil mixes with water underground during the shaking of an earthquake. The ground becomes very soft when the water and sediment mix, and it starts to behave like quicksand. After the earthquake is over, the water settles back where it came from deep underground, and the sediment becomes solid again.

> The liquid-rich soil below Mexico City is particularly susceptible to liquefaction, as shown by the 1985 earthquake, in which many buildings lost their support and collapsed.

DEADLY DATA

Most of the 10,000 people who died in the 1985 Mexico City earthquake were killed when the buildings they were in sank into liquefied sand.

How Earthquakes Measure Up

The shock waves that earthquakes create are violent and complex events. One way to understand them is by calculating their magnitude, which is a measure of the amount of energy they release. In the past, all earthquakes were measured using the Richter scale. Dr. Charles Richter, a seismologist at the California Institute of Technology, invented this scale in the 1930s. Today, the moment magnitude scale (MMS), or M scale, is more commonly used.

Minor earthquakes, with a magnitude of 1.5 or less, can happen in San Francisco every day!

The Richter Scale

The Richter scale was a measure of the largest seismic wave recorded on a particular kind of **seismometer** located about 62 miles (100 km) from the epicenter of an earthquake. A seismometer is a little like a pendulum on a fixed base. The rate at which the weight at the end of the pendulum swings can be used to record the shaking of Earth. This measurement is shown on a seismograph.

The scale of an earthquake can be measured by seismometers that show the shock waves on a graph like this.

The Magnitude Scale

Scientists devised the magnitude scale after the 1960 Chilean earthquake and the 1964 Alaskan earthquake. These earthquakes were so huge that the Richter scale did not adequately show the magnitude and size of what happened during these events. MMS more accurately measures the size of the shock waves during an earthquake. Each step in the scale is ten times greater than the previous number. The largest earthquake ever recorded on Earth was an M 9.5 quake, which occurred in Chile in 1960. The combined effects of the shock waves and tsunami it caused killed around 1,600 people, injured about 3,000, and left 2 million people homeless.

EARTH UNDER ATTACK! ▶ The amount of damage caused by an earthquake is measured by the Mercalli Scale, based on what people in the area feel and what damage they see to buildings around them. Mercalli scales are important to business and property owners in earthquake-affected areas.

Disaster Report: 2015, Nepal

When a massive earthquake ripped through Kathmandu Valley in Nepal on April 25, 2015, the country was shattered. This was the worst earthquake to hit Nepal for 80 years. It was made even more terrible by the fact that its epicenter was just 40 miles (64 km) away from the most densely populated part of the country, the capital city Kathmandu. Almost 9,000 people were killed, and it affected more than 8 million more, including many living in the remote, mountainous areas of the country.

The 2015 earthquake in Nepal flattened or damaged more than 850,000 homes, as well as schools, clinics, and other buildings.

The earthquake and its aftershocks damaged food and water supplies, and people struggled to find shelter and to get enough drinking water and food.

A Disaster Unfolds

Thousands of people were killed or badly injured when collapsing buildings or falling debris hit them. In Kathmandu, more than 1,000 people lost their lives. Deadly avalanches, like that which swept through Mount Everest base camp, buried people under a thick layer of snow. Tragically, many of Nepal's historic buildings were very badly damaged, including ancient temples and monuments.

Aftershocks!

One thing that made the quake so devastating was that its epicenter was relatively shallow, just 6 to 9 miles (10 to 14 km) below the ground, so that the shock waves at the surface were felt much more strongly. Deeper quakes have more earth to absorb the shaking. Not only that, but the main earthquake was followed by dangerous aftershocks. Most of these were small and, although frightening, caused only minor damage. However, the May 12 aftershock was as powerful as the main shock in a major earthquake. Many people slept in tents and shelters around Kathmandu for several weeks. They were afraid that if they stayed inside buildings, these might collapse if another shock struck.

EARTH UNDER ATTACK!

Nepal is vulnerable to earthquakes because of its position on the Alpides earthquake belt. Much of its tourism industry is based on people wanting to walk in or climb in the Himalayas, especially Mount Everest, which is becoming taller each year as a result of the convergent boundary miles beneath.

CHAPTER 5

AFTER THE QUAKE

The main shocks of most earthquakes last only seconds or minutes but for most people, the nightmare caused by these natural disasters is only just beginning. Earthquakes leave a trail of destruction and chaos in their wake, which can prove a challenge to even the wealthiest and best-equipped nations.

First on the Scene

The first priority is to rescue survivors and those people who are injured. They need to be taken to safety or to a hospital where their wounds can be treated. This is easier said than done. If an earthquake happens in a densely populated area, more people will be affected, and more buildings will be damaged. The time of day also has an impact. If a quake hits at night, more people will be in their homes sleeping, rather than on the move. More people could be buried under rubble from their homes in these cases. The weather can also make rescue and recovery more difficult. Heavy rains, high winds, or freezing conditions can make it harder for rescuers to do their work. Bad weather also puts casualties in greater danger, making it harder to reach them.

Rich and Poor

The biggest factor in the success of rescue operations is whether an earthquake hits a more economically or less economically developed country. Poorer countries have fewer **resources** and machinery to help them. This makes the work of rescuers much harder, for example, when telephone lines are down, and they do not have the technology that could help them communicate and coordinate their efforts. It may also mean they do not have the equipment that could help them shift vast amounts of rubble in a shattered city to reach survivors. If bridges have collapsed and roads have ripped apart, it can take a long time to repair these routes so that rescuers can reach victims, especially in remote or mountainous areas.

People can struggle for years to recover from the destruction earthquakes leave behind.

DEADLY DATA

The earthquake in Pakistan in 2005 killed more than 80,000 people and injured almost 70,000 more. Landslides, rockfalls, and collapsed buildings left 4 million people helpless for several days.

Rescue!

After an earthquake, emergency workers leap into action right away. Armed forces, firefighters, and search-and-rescue experts head to the scene to begin the difficult task of rescuing people trapped in buildings, cars, subways, and waterways. To reach victims, they may have to clear roads or rubble, or put out fires first, but their main aim is to get to those in need as fast and as safely as possible.

Search-and-rescue dogs help to locate survivors after the devastating earthquake in Van, Turkey, in 2011.

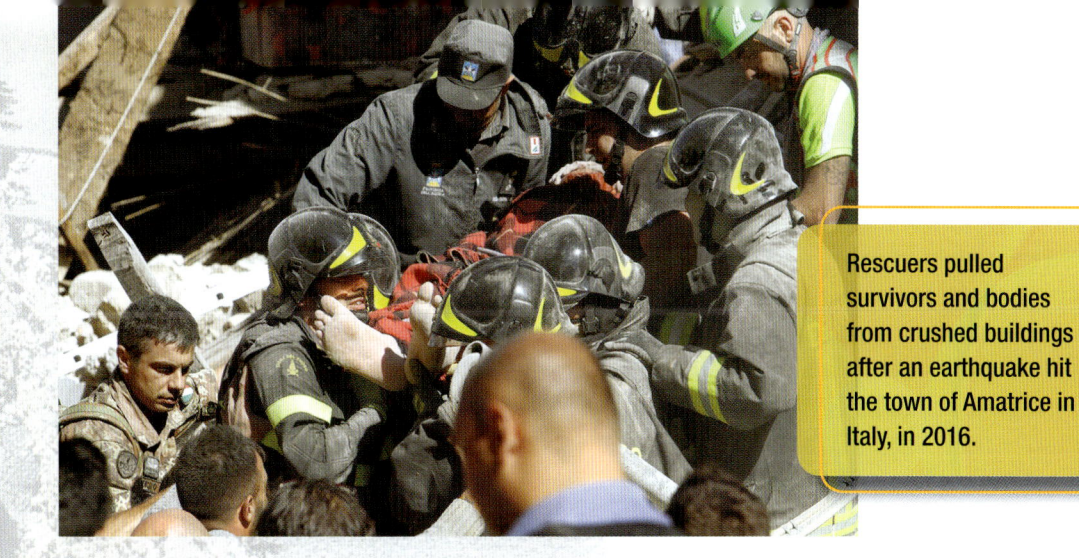

Rescuers pulled survivors and bodies from crushed buildings after an earthquake hit the town of Amatrice in Italy, in 2016.

Saving Survivors

Rescue workers often use sniffer dogs to smell hidden people. They may use special sound equipment that can detect the faintest of noises several yards away, to find people trapped under collapsed structures. To help spot survivors, they can also use video cameras fixed to the end of flexible poles that can squeeze through gaps in rubble. Rescue workers bring in heavy diggers as well as lifting and cutting equipment to remove the rubble and reach victims under crushed buildings or broken bridges. This is a delicate operation. One mistake, and rescuers could cause more rubble to collapse and endanger the lives of those they are seeking to help.

Help at Hand

Ambulances and medical staff are next to arrive at the earthquake site. They administer first aid to victims at the scene and take casualties to hospitals. Volunteers and workers from aid agencies, such as the American Red Cross, bring blankets and heaters to keep people warm, and supplies of food and water to keep survivors alive. They and government workers may also have to provide tents or shelters for people who have lost their homes. They also transport victims to temporary accommodation, such as town halls and gymnasiums. People stay in these places until they can be rehoused.

EARTH UNDER ATTACK!

It is hard to know when to stop searching for more survivors after an earthquake. Rescue efforts usually stop after five or seven days, when it is assumed that casualties will have died, but some people have survived for up to 13 days trapped beneath rubble if they have water.

Rebuilding Lives

When the dust has settled, casualties have been treated, and fires extinguished, a whole new wave of problems must be addressed. For one thing, an earthquake leaves behind huge areas of debris and rubble that have to be cleaned up and moved out of the way—for example, to free up streets and roads. Bulldozers are brought in to clear ruined buildings and structures, and sometimes, people set to work using hands and shovels only.

Health and Safety

Experts arrive to check that any buildings left standing really are safe for people to return to. They make sure that families can go back to the site to sift through the remains of their homes, salvaging what is left of their belongings. After a quake, water and sewage pipes may be damaged, so water becomes **contaminated**. Dirty floodwater may cover the land. This and the rotting waste left over from damaged stores and homes can cause disease, so this has to be dealt with, too. In some places, police officers may be brought in to keep people from **looting** stores and businesses left vulnerable while their owners are absent.

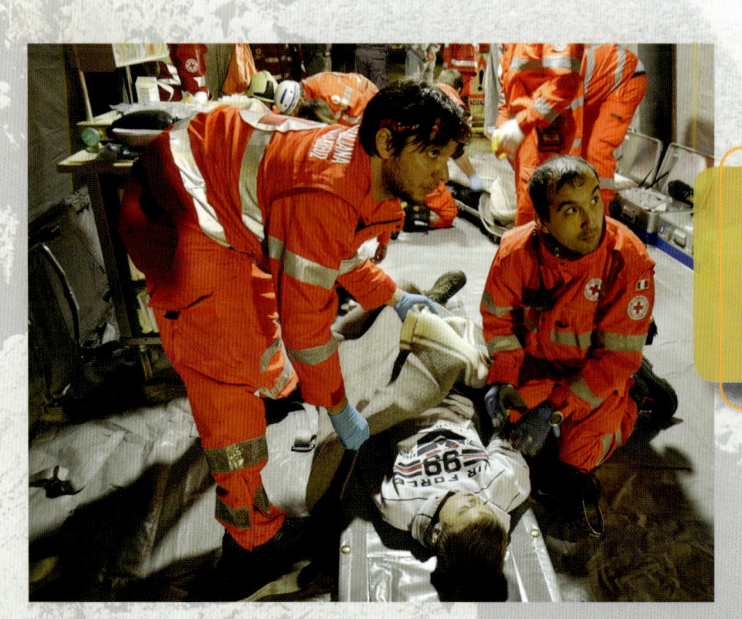

The first priority in any natural disaster is to find and treat any victims who are hurt and injured.

In Kathmandu, military forces help pull down damaged and dangerous buildings before rebuilding can start after the devastating earthquake of 2015.

Putting People First

Aid agencies and government organizations also help people who have become separated from their families or who cannot find family members. Many people lose their livelihoods in a natural disaster like an earthquake. Their store or farm may be destroyed, or their fishing boat may be washed away in a tsunami. They need money and help to restart their business in order to look after their families and rebuild their lives. When important landmarks, such as churches or temples, are lost, people may also want to rebuild these as soon as possible, because these are places religious people can find comfort.

DEADLY DATA

When a large earthquake was followed by 800 aftershocks in New Zealand in November 2016, the country's prime minister said it would cost billions of dollars to repair the roads, railroads, business, and homes damaged by the quake.

Disaster Report: 2010, Port-au-Prince, Haiti

Haiti's worst quake in more than 200 years struck the country in the late afternoon of January 12, 2010. The epicenter of the quake was just 15 miles (25 km) southwest of the Haiti's busy and densely populated capital city, Port-au-Prince. The disaster impacted the region of 3 million people, which accounts for one-third of the country's population, shocking and shaking the nation to its core.

Disaster Strikes

The Haiti earthquake was a large, M 7.0 event, made more damaging by the fact its epicenter was just 8 miles (13 km) below the surface. The earthquake shook the ground all over Haiti and the Dominican Republic and as far away as Cuba, Jamaica, and Puerto Rico. The disaster was also made worse by two large aftershocks, which immediately followed the main shock, and other aftershocks, which occurred more than a week later, on January 20.

A man stands in front of his house, which is being rebuilt after the 2010 earthquake in Haiti.

A large tent city stretches as far as the eye can see in Port-au-Prince, Haiti, 2010.

Hell for the Homeless

Port-au-Prince, home to 2.8 million people, suffered the worst damage and the most casualties. The buildings in this capital city were unable to cope with an earthquake of this magnitude. Across the country, 220,000 people were killed, and there were more than 300,000 casualties. In excess of 100,000 homes were destroyed, and 200,000 were seriously damaged. About 1 million people were left homeless, and after the quake, people were left living in tents. People urgently needed shelter, so tent camps were built because they were easy to assemble and fairly inexpensive. Unfortunately, the tents proved unsafe. Some people died because the tents could not withstand the rainy season when floods were common, and they collapsed. Others died because the tent camps were not supplied with sufficient clean water and toilets, which caused several disease outbreaks.

DEADLY DATA

Overall, around 1,200 tent camps sprang up all around the country, and because the country was slow to rehouse survivors, almost 400,000 people were still living in tents more than two years after the earthquake.

35

CHAPTER 6

LIVING IN A QUAKE ZONE

Worldwide, millions of people live in areas where there is a significant chance of experiencing a big earthquake. Why do people live in quake zones?

Coastal Living

Of the 23 biggest cities worldwide, 16 are on coasts. Of these, Los Angeles in the United States, Tokyo and Osaka in Japan, Shanghai in China, Manila in the Philippines, and Jakarta in Indonesia are in the Ring of Fire. These and other settlements have grown in this region for many reasons. There are harbors and ports for coastal trade. There are thriving coastal industries, such as fishing and tourism, focused on nearby beaches and islands. Often, coasts have mild climates and good weather, not to mention the beautiful sea views.

Fault Riches

Faults in a quake zone can be rich in resources. Volcanoes, often found on faults, bring magma to the surface. Over time, this turns into highly **fertile** soil that farmers can use to grow healthy, abundant crops. Rising magma at faults also pushes up gold formed underground. The famous Gold Rush, when thousands of miners descended on mountains near San Francisco in 1848, happened because gold had been found on the San Andreas fault. Faults can also supply free energy. Geothermal power comes from people pumping water underground to heat up. Back at the surface, the hot water is used to generate electricity and heat buildings. The crust at faults is often thin, so water is warmed by the mantle's intense heat at shallower depths than in other places.

People put up with the dangers of living in the Ring of Fire because of benefits such as work opportunities and quality of life.

DEADLY DATA

In Iceland, which is located on the mid-Atlantic fault, there are on average 150-400 earthquakes a week. The country gets one-quarter of its electricity and 90 percent of building heating from geothermal power.

Knowing Your Enemy

In quake zones, scientists try to reduce the impact of earthquake hazards by trying to understand their enemy better. For example, they develop and improve ways to monitor Earth to spot any changes that may be a sign of a forthcoming earthquake. Engineers reduce impacts by designing buildings and other structures that can cope with the shaking.

Early Warning Systems

Scientists have a number of different ways to try to predict when an earthquake will strike. The first is using a global network of seismometers to detect vibrations in Earth's crust. A rise in activity, with more frequent or larger episodes of shaking, can be a sign of an imminent quake.

Sensing Changes

The land surface can start to buckle and rise as stresses build deep underground. This is one sign that can warn scientists of a possible earthquake. Such gradual changes are often tricky to notice on the ground but easier in the air! **Satellites** in space can sense land surface changes using special sensors. The satellites send **radar** signals to Earth, and sensors record the strength of the signal reflected back to space from the land. It will be stronger on land closer to the satellite. Gases formed underground, such as radon, can escape through fine surface cracks preceding earthquakes. Scientists use sniffer robots to detect release of radon from the ground. A lot of radon could be a sign of an earthquake to come.

Changes to Earth sensed by satellites hundreds of miles above its surface are important tools in early warning of quakes.

Help from Animals

In 2009, nearly all male toads in an area left their breeding ponds just days before a large earthquake struck in Italy. In 1989, a scientist predicted a U.S. earthquake based partly on noticing newspaper ads reporting large numbers of pets disappearing in the days before the event. Some scientists and many other people believe that changes in animal behavior such as these can be used to predict earthquakes. Others believe it is just coincidence.

> Experts think that animals might be able to help predict earthquakes after toads were seen abandoning a pond in Italy, in 2009, days before a devastating earthquake.

DEADLY DATA

In 1975, when scientists spotted land height changes and increased seismic activity in a region of China, they ordered an evacuation. Within days, an M 7.3 earthquake struck the region. Although it killed more than 2,000 people, officials estimate it could have killed more than 150,000 with no evacuation. However, in 1976, a much more deadly quake of a similar strength struck nearby but with no changes in land height or seismic activity beforehand.

Quakeproof Buildings

The majority of people killed in an earthquake die because the building they are in collapses around them. That means that the number one way to reduce the death toll in an earthquake disaster is to construct buildings that are designed to withstand the violent shaking of the ground during a tremor. Of course, a very strong earthquake can still damage even the best-engineered house, but quakeproof buildings give people a better chance of survival.

Safer Buildings

A big issue is the choice of materials. If a building collapses, the people inside it have a better chance of survival if the walls and roof are made of lightweight materials instead of heavy ones. So, in a poorer country, where families cannot afford expensive, newer materials or designs, people could use different building materials or make those they use stronger. For example, mud houses often fall down in an earthquake because walls are not connected safely, and mud is a weak building material. Building strength can be improved simply by joining the edges of mud walls with a concrete-covered mesh wire. Safer still would be to build homes from wooden or steel frames, firmly attached together.

> The 49-story Transamerica pyramid building in San Francisco is wider at the bottom than the top. It has supports in its base to protect it from the shuddering ground in an earthquake.

Earthquake-resistant houses were built in 2007 after a large Earthquake hit central Java, Indonesia, in 2006.

Building Design

The design of a building also plays an important part. Engineers design buildings to withstand as much sideways motion as possible, in order to minimize damage to the structure and give the occupants time to get out safely. For example, engineers have built tall skyscrapers that float on systems of ball bearings, springs, or padded cylinders. These can act like shock absorbers in a car if an earthquake hits: They allow the building to sway a little with the quake, reducing the impact of the shaking ground on a building's foundations.

EARTH UNDER ATTACK!

The 2010 earthquake in Haiti was less powerful than one in Chile in that same year. While more than 200,000 died in Haiti, there were 700 fatalities in Chile. The difference was that in Haitian buildings had gone up quickly and cheaply, while the richer and more industrialized Chile had followed stricter and safer building regulations.

What to Do in an Earthquake

Earthquakes can happen at any time. There is no telling how big or bad they might be. People living in earthquake zones in particular should learn what to do if one strikes.

In Advance

One thing anyone in an earthquake zone should do, if they can, is to put together an emergency supply kit. This is a box or container that holds supplies a person may need in case of a disaster. It should include things such as water, food, a flashlight and extra batteries, a first-aid kit, a multipurpose tool, a cell phone with chargers, and blankets. Copies of personal documents, such as passports, birth certificates, insurance policies, and family and emergency contact information is also important. Families should also have an evacuation plan that includes knowing which safe place they should all go to. They should know who does what, for example, who is responsible for saving family pets. People should also keep up to date with local risk and response plans.

Children learn to protect their heads with books during an earthquake drill in a primary school in Greece.

This seismic forecasting system tower, with warning sirens, was erected after an underwater earthquake caused a tsunami in the Indian Ocean in 2004.

At the Time

When an earthquake hits, the first piece of advice is: Don't panic. This may be harder than it sounds, but it can save lives, since keeping calm allows people to remember what they should do. If someone is indoors, they should take cover under a strong table, desk, or doorframe, which could keep bricks and slates from falling on them. They should stay away from windows that could shatter and hurt them, and from furniture such as heavy bookcases, which could fall on them. People who are outdoors should run away from buildings because they might collapse, and from power lines and telephone wires that could electrocute them if they fall.

EARTH UNDER ATTACK!

After an earthquake, the disaster may continue. After the main shock, people should remember there may be dangerous aftershocks, so avoid returning to buildings at risk until these have passed. People should also expect and prepare for landslides or even a tsunami if they live on a coast, which can be set off by an earthquake.

Future Earthquakes

Earthquakes are a natural phenomenon that occur due to Earth's basic geological structure. The tectonic plates will keep shifting, causing pressure buildups that become earthquakes. If people live on a fault, then they will be at risk of earthquakes in the future.

Better Forecasts

A weather forecast is an educated guess about what might happen. These forecasts are based in part on visible patterns in Earth's **atmosphere** and oceans, such as clouds, which can mean rain. Earthquake forecasts are trickier. Shock wave and land surface changes depend, for example, on differences in the types, strengths, and thicknesses of rocks, as well as stress changes deep underground, far out of sight. Improvements in technology, such as better sensors of surface and deep planetary changes, should help scientists improve the accuracy of their earthquake predictions into the future.

Forecasts are based partly on the time since the last big quake happened and the presence of active faults. That is why scientists fear a major event in Tehran, Iran, in the Alpides belt, and they predict severe damage owing to the large numbers of poorly constructed homes.

Water seeping underground beneath big dams built to store water could increase the chance of earthquakes.

Man-Made Quakes

Some scientists believe that human activity can cause earthquakes. The worst culprit is pumping water deep underground. People do this to get rid of wastewater that contains harmful chemicals that might pollute drinking water. People pump fluids into oil and gas mines to wash out the oil and gas from holes in the rock. These liquids can make the rock of the crust in fault zones more likely to shift at faults. In the future, the world's growing population may need more fuel and reservoirs, and may create more wastewater. So, could our impact on the planet's crust cause more earthquakes? We need to remain vigilant and monitor the effect humans have on the planet to try and avoid future natural disasters.

DEADLY DATA

In the central United States, in each year from 1973 to 2008, there were around 20 earthquakes big enough to cause minor damage. However, wastewater injection since then has increased earthquake frequency. In 2014, there were 659 such earthquakes.

GLOSSARY

atmosphere the blanket of gases that surround Earth

atomic bomb the most powerful and destructive type of bomb

avalanches masses of snow, ice, and rocks sliding quickly down a mountainside

contaminated made dirty and often unsafe to use

convergent where two tectonic plates move together

dams structures built to trap water in a reservoir

divergent where two tectonic plates pull apart

fault the place where two or more different tectonic plates meet

fertile containing nutrients that promote growth of plants

friction the force that slows down an object when it is moving against another object or material

geologists scientists who study what Earth is made of and how it formed

geology the study of what Earth is made of and how it formed

hazards dangers or risks

landslide a mass of rock and soil sliding down a slope

levees raised walls that prevent flooding of a river or other body of water

looting stealing, especially in times of war or natural disaster

magma liquid, hot rock found underground that can exit at volcanoes as lava

mudslides masses of mud sliding down a slope

plateau area of raised but level high ground

radar a system using radio waves to locate objects at a distance

reservoir a man-made lake

resources things that people need or use, such as oil and freshwater

Ring of Fire the earthquake and volcano belt that circles the Pacific Ocean

rupture to break or crack open

rural having to do with the countryside

satellites objects people put in space that can take photos of Earth

sediment material made of small or fine particles, such as mud or sand

seismologists scientists who study earthquakes

seismometer a machine that measures the shaking of the ground during a volcano or earthquake

shock waves the spreading vibration through a substance, for example, caused by an earthquake

strike-slip fault the fault at a transform boundary

tectonic plates large sections of Earth's crust floating on the mantle

transform where two tectonic plates slide past each other

volcanic eruptions when pressure forces magma or hot gases out of volcanoes

FOR MORE INFORMATION

BOOKS

Elizabeth, Elkins. *Investigating Earthquakes* (Investigating Natural Disasters). Chicago, IL: Capstone Press, 2017.

Furgan, Kathy. *Everything Volcanoes and Earthquakes* (National Geographic Kids). Washington, DC: National Geographic Children's Books, 2013.

Owens, Meredith P. *Earthquakes* (Spotlight on Earth Science). New York, NY: PowerKids Press, 2017.

Perish, Patrick. *Survive an Earthquake* (Survival Zone). Minnetonka, MN: Torque, 2017.

WEBSITES

Learn more about the science of earthquakes at:
earthquake.usgs.gov/learn/kids/eqscience.php

Want to know more about how earthquakes work? Go to:
science.howstuffworks.com/nature/natural-disasters/earthquake.htm

Watch this National Geographic video about earthquakes at:
video.nationalgeographic.com/video/101-videos/earthquake-101

Meet Eddy, who knows a lot about earthquakes at:
www.onegeology.org/extra/kids/earthquakes.html

Publisher's note to educators and parents: Our editors have carefully reviewed these websites to ensure that they are suitable for students. Many websites change frequently, however, and we cannot guarantee that a site's future contents will continue to meet our high standards of quality and educational value. Be advised that students should be closely supervised whenever they access the Internet.

INDEX

Alpides 16, 17, 18, 27, 44
avalanches 7, 27

buildings 4, 6, 7, 12, 13, 19, 20, 22, 23, 25, 27, 28, 29, 30, 31, 32, 33, 35, 36, 37, 40–41, 43

Chile 15, 25, 41
convergent boundaries 10, 14, 27
crust 8, 9, 10, 14, 17, 36, 38, 45

divergent boundaries 10

emergency supply kit 42
emergency workers 30
epicenter 20, 24, 26, 27, 34

faults 10, 11, 14, 18, 36, 37, 44, 45
fire 6, 7, 30, 32
floods 6, 7, 13, 32, 35
foreshocks 20
friction 11

geologists 18
geology 20
geothermal power 36, 37

Haiti 34–35, 41
houses 13, 31, 34, 35, 40, 41

Indonesia 36, 41
inner core 8, 9

landslides 6, 7, 12, 29, 43
liquefaction 22, 23
looting 32

magma 8, 15, 36
magnitude 16, 24–25, 35
main shock 20, 21, 27, 28, 34, 43
mantle 8, 9, 15, 36
Mercalli Scale 25
mid-ocean ridges 10
moment magnitude scale (MMS) 24, 25
mountains 7, 16–17, 19, 26, 28, 36
mudslides 7

Nepal 5, 16–17, 26–27
North Anatolian fault 18

outer core 8, 9

Pacific Ocean 14
Pakistan 16, 29

radar 38
resources 28, 36
Richter, Dr. Charles 24
Richter scale 24–25
rift valleys 10
Ring of Fire 14, 15, 16, 36, 37

San Andreas fault 11, 36
satellites 38
sediment 22, 23
seiches 13
seismic waves 20, 24
seismograph 24
seismologists 8, 24
seismology 8
seismometers 24, 25, 38
shock waves 20–21, 23, 24, 25, 27, 44
strike-slip fault 11, 14
subsidence 6

tectonic plates 8, 10–11, 13, 14, 15, 16, 17, 18, 19, 44
transform boundaries 10, 11, 14
tremors 11, 22–23, 40
tsunami 12–13, 25, 33, 43
Turkey 18–19, 30

volcanoes 15, 36